D0780458

Pebble® Plus

AFRICAN ANIMALS
Giraffes

by Catherine Ipcizade
Consulting Editor: Gail Saunders-Smith, PhD

Consultant:
George Wittemyer, PhD
NSF International Postdoctoral Fellow
University of California at Berkeley

Capstone press®

Mankato, Minnesota

Pebble Plus is published by Capstone Press,
151 Good Counsel Drive, P.O. Box 669, Mankato, Minnesota 56002.
www.capstonepress.com

1 2 3 4 5 6 13 12 11 10 09 08

Library of Congress Cataloging-in-Publication Data
Ipcizade, Catherine.
    Giraffes / by Catherine Ipcizade.
    p. cm. — (Pebble plus. African animals)
    Includes bibliographical references and index.
    ISBN-13: 978-1-4296-1246-3 (hardcover)
    ISBN-10: 1-4296-1246-0 (hardcover)
    1. Giraffe — Africa — Juvenile literature. I. Title. II. Series.
QL737.U56I73 2008
599.638 — dc22   2007028676

Summary: Discusses giraffes, their African habitat, food, and behavior.

Editorial Credits
Erika L. Shores, editor; Renée T. Doyle, set designer; Laura Manthe, photo researcher

Photo Credits
Afripics.com, 16–17
Digital Vision/Jeremy Woodhouse, 14–15
fotolia/Luc Patureau, 6–7
Gerry Ellis, 4–5
Getty Images Inc./Art Wolfe, 11; Roy Toft, 12–13
iStockphoto/Richard Fitzer, cover
Photodisc/Siede Preis, cover, 1, 3 (fur)
Shutterstock/Chris Anderson, 18–19; Christian Musat, 22; Marina Cano Trueba, 8–9; Tebenkova Svetlana, 20–21;
    Ursula, 1

The author dedicates this book to her husband, her children, and her nieces and nephew —
keep dreaming, keep believing.

Note to Parents and Teachers

The African Animals set supports national science standards related to life science.
This book describes and illustrates giraffes. The images support early readers in
understanding the text. The repetition of words and phrases helps early readers learn
new words. This book also introduces early readers to subject-specific vocabulary words,
which are defined in the Glossary section. Early readers may need assistance to read
some words and to use the Table of Contents, Glossary, Read More, Internet Sites, and
Index sections of the book.

Table of Contents

Living in Africa

Africa is hot!
Giraffes like living on
the hot, grassy savanna.

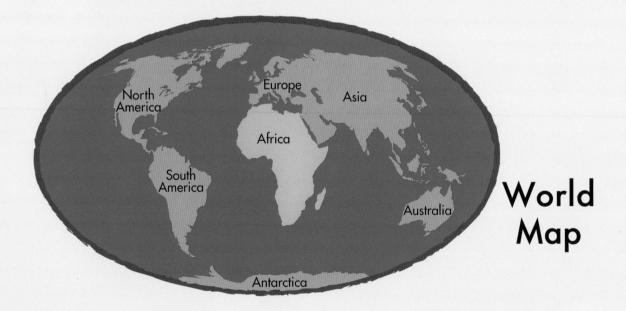

North
America

Europe

Asia

Africa

South
America

Australia

Antarctica

World
Map

Giraffes run through grasses
on the flat land.
They stay cool
under tall savanna trees.

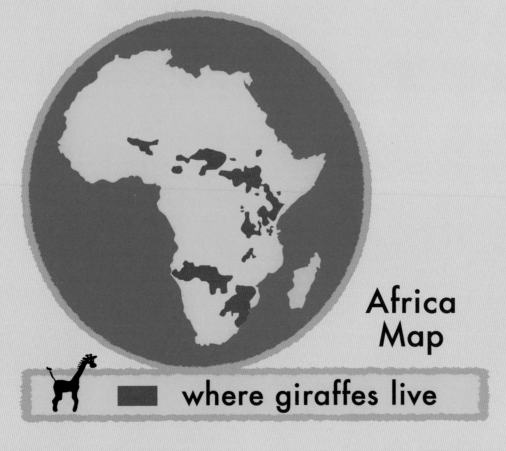

Africa
Map

where giraffes live

Up Close!

A giraffe's spots
are like fingerprints.
No two giraffes have
the same pattern of spots.

Look at that long tongue!

A giraffe's blue tongue

is as long as your arm.

Eating and Drinking

Giraffes stretch up high

to eat leaves

on the tallest trees.

Giraffes bend down low
for a drink of water.
Giraffes can go days
between drinks.

Staying Safe

Is that a hungry lion?

Lions hunt giraffes.

Giraffes use their long legs

to outrun danger.

Female giraffes keep

the calves safe in a herd.

Mother giraffes

will kick enemies

to scare them away.

Giraffes often sleep standing

on their big, round hooves.

They keep one eye open

to look for danger.

Good night, giraffes.

Glossary

calf — a young giraffe; more than one calf is calves.

danger — something that is not safe

fingerprint — the mark made by the tip of the finger; no two people have the same fingerprints.

hoof — the hard covering over the foot of a giraffe; more than one hoof is hooves.

pattern — a repeating order of colors and shapes

savanna — a flat, grassy plain with few trees

Read More

Anderson, Jill. *Giraffes*. Wild Ones. Minnetonka, Minn.: Northword Press, 2005.

Helget, Nicole. *Giraffes*. Living Wild. Mankato, Minn.: Creative Education, 2008.

Parker, Barbara Keevil. *Giraffes*. Early Bird Nature Books. Minneapolis: Lerner, 2005.

Internet Sites

FactHound offers a safe, fun way to find Internet sites related to this book. All of the sites on FactHound have been researched by our staff.

Here's how:

1. Visit *www.facthound.com*

2. Choose your grade level.

3. Type in this book ID **1429612460** for age-appropriate sites. You may also browse subjects by clicking on letters, or by clicking on pictures and words.

4. Click on the **Fetch It** button.

FactHound will fetch the best sites for you!

Index

Word Count: 137
Grade: 1
Early-Intervention Level: 16